HOME SERIES
CONTEMPORARY HOUSES

BETA-PLUS

HOME SERIES

CONTENTS

P. 4-5
The interior of this house by architect Marc Verstraeten was created by Philip Simoen. Flexform sofas around a Mario Botta table. Wide solid oak floorboards.

P. 6
This living room alongside the dining room was designed by RR Intérieur.
Flexform sofa (Ground Piece). In the background, a solid oak table created by RR Intérieur. Lamp by Bart Lens. Piet chairs by Piet Boon and a Palomino rug from Limited Edition.

INTRODUCTION

I n contemporary style, progress is a matter of living in symbiosis with the architecture and furniture of the age, but at the same time facing resolutely towards the future. Understatedness, clean lines, neutral tones, innovative materials – these are the typical signs of a contemporary interior. This book illustrates current architectural trends through some fifteen creations by top-level architects and interior decorators. These accounts prove that the modern way of life requires much more than harmonious integration of cutting-edge furniture design into a modern context. Whether a new build or a renovation project, the project manager, the architects and the interior specialists work on a complex mix of volumes and perspectives, lights and atmospheres, materials and textures, shapes and colours.

Here, purely cerebral architectural bravura can be found, and the inhabitants appreciate each space in these homes, day after day.

There are many examples of the art of contemporary living: the modern atmosphere of an old country house; the stunning metamorphosis of a historic farmhouse; the serene, clean shapes of a present-day dwelling; the minimalist power of glass and brick dwellings; the perfect composition and harmony of colours in recently created apartments, and more.

P. 8
This bathroom with its clean lines is covered in white Carrara marble in a house created by the architect Baudouin Courtens.

P. 10-11
A kitchen in solid oak (floor covering, table and benches) in a house designed by Vlassak-Verhulst.

OASIS OF SPACE

The dining room opens impressively onto the garden, thanks to the striking space created by immense picture windows. The oak floor has been bleached.

T he Schellen architect practice created the architecture and interior of this contemporary villa, surrounded by lush greenery.

Linda Coart designed the interior to emphasise an alliance between the interior and exterior and reveal an oasis of space.

Uncluttered understatement produces a whole that meets the eye without complications. There are few decorative objects – the furniture is used for both its function and its aesthetic quality. Luminous, simple architecture. A range of highly understated colours decorates the whole house: the walls are primarily in white, with some in grey or black.

The long gas fireplace set into the black wall dominates the living room,
from which you can also see the bookcase and the multimedia area.
A high wooden sliding wall allows the room some privacy.

The kitchen looks out onto the garden. A large canopy is an invitation to eat outside. The central unit with its work surface and sink are in stainless steel. All the kitchen appliances are brought together in a single block. Enamelled glass is used for the oven splashboard.

The office overlooking the space forms a central area that offers a panoramic view over the magnificent garden.

In the bathroom, all eyes are drawn to the Boffi bath with its basins and its matching taps. The walls of the shower feature the Cotto d'Este tiles chosen for the kitchen and entrance hall.

RADICAL TRANSFORMATION

OF A 1959 VILLA

T his section presents a recent project by architect Olivier Dwek in a wooded quarter of Brussels.

This classic 1959 villa has been completely remodelled and transformed. The renovation works took two years: several walls were demolished and the spatial layout underwent a complete metamorphosis.

The refinement of the interior layout contributes to the serene atmosphere of the place: only high-quality, warm materials were chosen, such as natural Portuguese stone, a tinted wooden floor, exclusive leather and velvet covers, silk curtains, etc.

The intentionally limited harmony of colour (dominated by browns and greys) also accentuates the restful atmosphere of the whole ensemble.

All the sofas, footstools, low tables, the day bed, armchairs, shagreen seats and benches were designed by architect and interior designer Caroline Notté and produced by Vanhamme.

This day bed was designed by Caroline Notté and covered in a Donghia fabric in flamed linen velvet with coffee-coloured highlights.

The monumental entrance hall is inspired by the Guggenheim Museum in New York. Sculpture by Tony Cragg.

P. 24-25

In the background, two velveteen armchairs from Marie's Corner with seating cushions in full-grain anthracite leather. To their left, two shagreen seats in natural leather. The long-weave rug was made to measure from pure wool. Indirect lighting has been built into the suspended ceiling.

The sofa to the left of the photo (nearly 4m long) is covered in velveteen from Marie's Corner. The bench on the left of the open fireplace is made from "China red" silk velvet. The low U-shaped table is made of wenge wood.

The floor of the entrance hall is made of natural Portuguese Azul Cascais stone. The curved, bevelled skirting, locally made, is a mark of the passion for detail of the project's designer and creators.

The main desk of the house and the console table, both in tinted oak, were designed by Olivier Dwek. The canvas is by Italian painter Flavio Piras.

The games room is lit using "Icebox" suspended lighting from Tal. The artwork is by German artist Andreas Bitesnich. Silk drapes.

P. 28
The all-stainless steel laundry, inspired by industrial kitchens, was created by Olivier Dwek. Here again, natural Portuguese Azul Cascais stone was chosen for the flooring.

The loft-style guest bedroom. The head of the bed consists of an arching wall that provides double access to the bathroom.

P. 30
The colossal bookcase was made to measure on two levels with a gangway by Olivier Dwek in collaboration with Claire Bataille.

The staircase and all the floors of the house are made of high-quality tinted oak.

The access corridor to the lower part of the bookcase and a lounge area. The suspended ceiling creates indirect atmospheric light. Primitive sculptures from South Africa.

EQUILIBRIUM AND TIMELESS

ATMOSPHERE

 villa built in the 1950s has been transformed by the interior architect's office P&M Projects.

It now leans towards contemporary architecture, tempered by a few pieces of antique furniture.

The palette of colours and materials is testimony to a clear, balanced, timeless line.

Simple surroundings for the living room in neutral tones. The light-coloured floor and the shape and understated nature of the furniture give this area a serene atmosphere.

The entrance hall, laid with Pietra Piasentina stone, is the main artery to all the vital areas of the house.

Warmer surroundings in the kitchen and dining room, with the main wall painted purple, alongside raw oak – providing a natural finish for the made to measure furniture.
Work surfaces in ash grey-yellow Buxy stone.

The bedroom and dressing room form a cosy ensemble. This is followed by the bathroom and a suite of adjoining bedrooms.

PERFECT UNION OF CONTEMPORARY

AND CLASSICAL DESIGN

R Intérieur, an interior design store of over 2000 m^2 in the seaside town of Knokke-le-Zoute, not only offers a vast range of contemporary designer furniture: Rik Ruebens and his team also advise visitors on creating and decorating their homes.

Their concept? Bringing together contemporary and classical collections in each project to create interiors with low-key elegance and unique charisma.

P. 40-41
RR Intérieur designed the interior decoration for this seaside villa: an informal mix consisting of a modern interior in a timeless setting.
Flexform Resort corner living room suite.

A Poliform Sintesi desk with a Pausa (Flexform) chair.

A Maat solid oak table with matching bench.

P. 44-45
Solid oak dining room table. Bart Lens
lamp, Piet Boon chairs and Palomino rug
from Limited Edition.

P. 46-47
Flexform armchairs (Groundpiece model)
around a Brera coffee table from
Casamilano. Thomas armchairs from
Flexform.

An open Ubik dressing room from Poliform and a Boston wardrobe, also from Poliform.

View of the new garden furniture collection by the Dutch designer Piet Boon: table, love-seat and daybed.

UNDERSTATED REFINEMENT

IN A HIGH-TECH ENVIRONMENT

In this home, designed by Marc Corbiau for a young family with three children, Stéphanie Laporte from The Office was responsible for the interior decoration. She worked in close collaboration with Obumex for this project. The austerity of the general lines gives a Zen touch to this apartment.

The owners were looking for a home that was practical, simple and pleasant to live in. Stéphanie Laporte opted to use clear and understated, comfortable decoration, bathed in natural light and created using very tough materials: dark, natural stone for the floor and the washbasin unit in the cloakroom; tinted, brushed oak veneer for the wardrobes and solid oak flooring.

The lighting also plays an important role and great attention was paid to home automation and new audio and video techniques, lighting control, security, video phone solutions and climate control using touch screens, internet and made to measure control panels (design and implementation by Dubois Ctrl – air conditioning and automation concepts).

P. 50-51
The made to measure solid oak staircase is the same shade as the floor.
The furniture and cupboards in the office were designed to measure by Devaere. Promemoria lamp (from Obumex) and fully integrated climate control (note the understated openings in the ceiling).
The washbasin unit in the cloakroom, in natural stone, was made to measure by Guido Herman. Vola taps.

All the furniture and lighting in the living room come from Promemoria. Bruder linen curtains, Crestron touch screen and Dubois Ctrl touch panel.

Christian Liaigre chairs surround a Promemoria table (all from Obumex). A special stucco painting technique was applied on the walls. Vases by Gunther Lambert.

Maximum discretion and understatement in this almost invisible kitchen. Its presence is betrayed only by the oven and the sink. A good way to integrate a kitchen into an open space.

Natural stone, oak veneer and stainless steel intermingle in the kitchen. The refrigerator is integrated into the storage. Bruder wooden slats.

View from the landing (with Fred Boffin artworks) towards the bedroom, entirely decorated in oak veneer. Bruder curtains, bed frame from Dubois Ctrl.

Bisazza glass mosaic, natural stone and oak veneer were chosen for the bathroom.

The dressing room is also decorated in oak veneer.

The staircase to the second floor was designed to measure in solid oak; shot-blasted stainless steel parts.

A DESIGNER HOUSE

IN A CLEAN-CUT STYLE

C larity, whiteness and symmetry for this interior by Bruce Bananto, the famous New York interior architect.

For this project, he worked with EA2 (European Architectural Antiques), an international company that specialises in historic European building materials. The result is a minimalist mixture of European and American stylistic elements in a house with an uncluttered design.

Monochrome white in an understated setting, created by interior architect Bruce Bananto.

The Colonial-style American open fireplace has been replaced by a minimalist porcelain wall, provided by EA2.

The small antique table with its original patina comes from Sweden.

P. 62-63
On the left, the white wall has been given a gloss finish to contrast with the other walls: a perfectly applied gloss that accentuates the contemporary atmosphere. The armchairs in the foreground are Gerrit Rietveld creations. The white coffee table is Italian-made. To the right, two Bruce Bananto chairs. Bruder Hemp rug.

The kitchen was designed by Boston architect Bruce A. Wood.
The chairs are the work of Italian designer Gio Ponti. The Corian stainless steel unit is a Bananto piece.

The long dining room table was designed by Bruce Bananto and made to measure by EA2 in bleached oak boards. Mario Bellini chairs.

AT HOME IN THE HEART OF ART

russels architect Olivier Dwek
has created the ideal home for
a couple of passionate art-
lovers. It is an old rustic cottage transformed into a contemporary showcase,
housing a collection of modern art that
is naturally integrated.

The interior space has been fully opened
up to make the most of the light and
perspectives, and to re-establish contact
with the surrounding natural environment. This project was developed in collaboration with architect Mathieu
Dewitte.

In the hall, Olivier Dwek has created a
powerful feeling of space by removing
the stair rail and opening up the hall
onto the living room and garden. The
pedestal bears a sculpture of Belgian
author Charles Plisnier, by Akarova. A
series of Plaster Surrogates by Allan
McCollum are hung above the stairs.

The family room, with a sofa designed by Stéphanie Parein. Stools by Eero Saarinen for Knoll. The dark tones of this room contrast with the rest of the house.

An artwork by Robert Rauschenberg in the hall.

The LC2 armchairs in the living room are the work of Le Corbusier. The coffee table and chairs are by Christian Liaigre. The dark, exotic wood floor has been treated with natural matt. Here again, modern art is at the forefront: a blue sculpture by Yves Klein, a column by Koen Theys, a collage by Korean artist Wang and a photograph by Bustami.

The kitchen, designed by Olivier Dwek, was built by Bulthaup. Black doors and a very thin work surface (10 mm) in stainless steel. Delta Light spotlights. The black monochrome canvas is by Sol LeWitt.

The bedroom ensuite is located on a lower level than the dressing room that overlooks the mirror wall.
The washbasins and bath have no visible joints: they have the appearance of independent, monolithic blocks. Bathroom designed by Dwek, with Vola taps.

A TO Z COORDINATION

The company De Lobo Interior Surrounds You is the fruit of designer Tom De Wulf's association with the Van Poucke office (interior design).

In this section, they present the renovation of a large historical farmhouse converted into a dwelling with contemporary architecture. False ceilings, furniture with understated, clean lines, and fashionable 'broken', subtle colours.

A successful metamorphosis: this current and modern interpretation reveals a cosy interior with timeless elegance.

Pivoting doors lead from the corridor into the living areas.
To the left, shoe storage, and to the right, access to the wine cellar. The floor to ceiling partition walls bring calm and serenity.

On the mezzanine, a bookcase between the reading corner and working space. Furniture made to measure and floor in wenge wood.

Contrast of materials in the dining room: a large oak table beside black leather armchairs.

A chic, elegant wine cellar with oak cases.

The kitchen consists of an island and a partition wall to hide all the appliances. The work surfaces in yellow Massangis are mitred to accentuate the purity of the lines. The floor is made of natural Bourgogne stone, produced by Van den Bogaert Leon.

The bedroom. The bed and the large wardrobe are made to measure entirely out of dark oak. Gas fireplace from De Puydt.

MINIMALISM AT EASE

This house, located in one of the green quarters of Brussels, was designed by architect Jean-Marie Gillet with an interior by designer Jacques Van Haren, who describes this project as the "Essential House": a house where all of life's functions are reduced to their essence and reformed into one great whole.

A modern, utterly clean-lined space thanks to a geometric aesthetic that has been taken to the extreme. Exclusively white walls with discreet floors for total austerity throughout.

The sunken living room offers an excellent view of the garden. The seat covering was chosen to match the accents of natural stone. A suspended table and ultrafine steel chairs, covered in ebony.

The main furniture has been created in ebony. The Panama stools
are by Jacques Van Haren. The floor is natural Bateig stone. The
cross-shaped pillars are a reference to Mies van der Rohe's
pavilion in 1939.

Bathroom in glass and natural stone: Bateig stone for the furniture and lava stone as the wall covering. The dome and the windows have electrochromatic glass. The windows open electronically and disappear into the walls.

Separate dressing room for guests in the entrance hall. The concrete floor was coloured in the mixing stage.

The master bedroom, with a large glass partition wall to the left. The stone bed head also serves as a washbasin on the bathroom side. The sliding wall allows plenty of light to enter the room and supports a pharmacy cabinet in the bathroom.

The guest bedroom, also bathed in light.

UNITING ANCIENT AND MODERN

A n entire floor (around 220 m²) of an old factory has been transformed and redesigned as a contemporary loft by interior architect Yvonne Hennes.

The owner was essentially looking for a light-filled, functional atmosphere.

Yvonne Hennes opted for an understated, timeless arrangement, whilst highlighting the existing structure. The juxtaposition of these rustic architectural elements with modern decoration sets the rhythm for this original interior with unique charm.

A lift provides direct access to the apartment. A partition that stops short of the ceiling separates the entrance from the living room. It ensures the intimacy of the living room while giving a hint of the scale of the space. The cloakroom block is suspended in this partition. From the living room side, it is the home of an antique dresser and Bang & Olufsen hi-fi system.

P. 90-91
The loft floor is covered in bleached oak flooring. The living room furniture, table and chairs are from Maxalto.

The kitchen area, integrated into the living room, was designed by Yvonne Hennes. It has been created using painted MDF panels.

The bathroom is separated from the bedroom by a sliding door. Here again, the same contemporary, light, youthful state of mind is apparent. A stool and a chair from the old factory recall the unique character of the place.

ONLY LIGHT

The house of architect Pascal François is a very understated, simple brick structure. To accentuate its form, the opening at the entrance has been cut out with a precision bordering on surgical.

The entire surface of the façade has been covered in immaculate, smooth white plaster for insulation.

Light is the primary decorative element of this interior. It's everywhere, structuring, revealing and giving life to the space.

View of the private staircase, with glass artwork by Anna Torfs in the foreground.

The concrete staircase leads to the design studio of the architect's office.

The chimney, a Pascal François design, was produced by De Puydt. The large glass frame brings inside and outside together.
In the living room there is a 7 m high space.
The side table displays glass work by Anna Torfs.

A "Jan" table in wenge wood by Emmemobili.
At the back, a white sideboard with two sliding elements surrounding a wenge centre is used for storage.

P. 98
The kitchen has two concrete elements: the first, a U-shape around the sink unit, the second, a work surface in the cooking area.

View from the living room towards the dining room and kitchen.
Once more, the glass work placed on the cabinet provides a note of colour.

A CLASSIC "BEL ÉTAGE"

TURNED INTO LOFT SPACE

A rchitect Benoît Bladt and the Kultuz office have made this house into a 21stcentury version of the classic "bel étage", in which the living room is traditionally located on the first floor.

The open spaces do not communicate with each other horizontally as usual, but instead vertically, thanks to the huge frames and open staircases. This minimalist loft has a note of relative sweetness thanks to its warm oak floor.

The red painted wall connects the dining room with the living room and gives both rooms character.

The choice of underfloor heating means that radiators can be dispensed with and an uncluttered structure is possible. The glass balustrade around the space looking down to the lower level creates a good view throughout the house from every spot.

The kitchen design, which is architecturally integrated into the house, is thanks to Kultuz. The clean lines accentuate the impression of space.

The absence of joints in the smooth floor covering and the simplicity of the concept chosen for the bathroom and office reinforce cohesion across the whole ensemble.

P. 104
The open staircases allow light to reach the heart of the house.

A VAST PENTHOUSE

IN SUBTLE SHADES

P hilip Simoen was asked to design the interior of this penthouse, which is over 350 m².

The result highlights this interior architect's preference for understated, yet warm environments: the subtle colour nuances are in harmony with noble materials (natural stone, silk velvet, bronze, tinted oak, etc.) in a refined, contemporary environment.

The hall floor is entirely covered in a grey-tinted oak floorboards (Vanrobaeys). The console table was made to measure. Lola lighting.

Maxalto sofas and small bronze tables from Promemoria around a coffee table, also from Promemoria. The open fireplace was produced by De Puydt. All the cupboards are made to measure.

A Maxalto table with Promemoria chairs (Caffè model). The kitchen was created by Wilfra in wenge and white formica. Granito work surface. Kitchen chairs by B&B Italia.

P. 110-111
Promemoria armchairs; covers in silk velvet. Bookcase cabinets made to measure in bleached, sanded oak. Curtains by Romo (Linara), made by Inndekor. Gas fireplace by De Puydt.

This large room includes work space, living room and bookcase. Made to measure in tinted oak, the desk is the work of Philip Simoen. The bronze table lamp and the standing lamps are by Christian Liaigre.

The main bedroom, with a Promemoria bed and armchair. Liaigre lighting. The chest of drawers under the plasma screen was designed by Philip Simoen and made from tinted oak. The dressing room is also the work of Philip Simoen.

LIGHT, SYMMETRY

AND UNDERSTATEMENT

This contemporary house was built after the owners fell in love with one of the last available plots of land with an open outlook in a residential area bordering a forest, surrounded by century-old trees.

The project was entrusted to Baudouin Courtens architect's practice. The owners wanted a family home open to the outside, with a focus on light, symmetry and understatedness.

To bring these wishes to life, Sophie Campion has created a combination where the understated nature of the materials and the warmth of the neutral base colours takes precedence. Harmony reigns in every room. The selection of African artworks reflects a search for nobility and rawness. The ever-present wood is the guiding theme running through all the rooms and the key element in an overall cosy atmosphere.

The living room opens onto the hall, the dining room and the office come multimedia area through high sliding doors in grey-tinted brushed oak. The three rooms open onto the garden and can be partitioned off as desired. Linen curtains. Two Chinese chests of drawers mark the entrance to the dining room. The leather footstool is by Christian Liaigre. Sculpture by Olivier Strebelle, flouting Yoruba mythology.

The entrance hall in Pietra Piasentina sets the pace for the passage to all the ground floor rooms and the intentionally discreet stairwell, leading to the mezzanine gangway to the bedrooms and the owners' apartment. Lola wall lights by Liaigre.

P. 116-117
You enter the living room through two brushed oak sliding doors, which divide the ground floor. Interni sofa. The rosewood and steel console table marks the boundary between the living room area and the area leading towards the dining room and the office. Orange China linen low chairs and a small Hurel table.

P. 118-119
The office-cum-audiovisual area is marked by the olive brown oak panelling. The warm atmosphere is brought out by the shade of the panelling and the bookcase. A Hurel sofa with silk cushions by Jim Thompson. A low ebony table. All audiovisual equipment is hidden behind a sliding door.

The grey oak panels create the warmer atmosphere of the dining room. Each cupboard opens along the deep join running the length of the panels. The dining room table was made to measure, together with the suspended lamps. The table bears a brushed sycamore bowl by Ernst Gamperi.

P. 120
The panelling detail. Hurel armchair in orange linen and silk by Jim Thompson. On the right, a footstool in smooth velvet. Shamba crest.

The kitchen was created by Obumex in grey tinted oak. Floor and work surfaces in Pietra Piasentina. Stools by Claire Bataille.

The dressing room and bedroom are separated by a pivoting panel in tinted brushed oak that, once closed, disappears as part of the U-shaped panelling of the bedroom. The central furniture piece consists of drawers and is leather-covered, as is the window seat. All the wood leaves were selected and assembled especially.

HOME SERIES

Volume 13 : CONTEMPORARY HOUSES

The reports in this book are selected from the Beta-Plus collection of home-design books: www.betaplus.com
They have been compiled in a special series by Le Figaro in French language: Ma Déco

Copyright © 2009 Beta-Plus Publishing / Le Figaro
Originally published in French language

PUBLISHER
Beta-Plus Publishing
Termuninck 3
B – 7850 Enghien
Belgium
www.betaplus.com
info@betaplus.com

TEXT
Alexandra Druesne

PHOTOGRAPHY
Jo Pauwels

DESIGN
Polydem - Nathalie Binart

TRANSLATIONS
Txt-Ibis

ISBN : 978-90-8944-044-0

Printed in China

P. 126-127
A design by interior architect Philip Simoen.
Architecture: Marc Verstraeten.